let the dead in

let the dead in

saida agostini

Alan Squire Publishing
Bethesda, Maryland

let the dead in is published by Alan Squire Publishing, Bethesda, MD

© 2022 Saida Agostini

All rights reserved. Except for brief passages quoted in newspaper, magazine, online, radio, or television reviews, no part of this book may be reproduced in any form or by any means, electronic or mechanical, including photocopying or recording, or by any information storage and retrieval system, without permission in writing from the publisher (www.AlanSquirePublishing.com).

Printed in the United States of America
ISBN (print): 978-1942892-28-1
ISBN (epub): 978-1942892-29-8

Library of Congress Control Number: 2021917706

Cover painting by Stephen Towns, *All Is Vanity*
Jacket design by Randy Stanard, Dewitt Designs
Author photo by Dorret Oosterhoff
Copy editing and interior design by Nita Congress
Printing consultant: Steven Waxman
Printed by Cushing-Malloy

First Edition
Ordo Vagorum

For Fanny, Joyce, and Anne

Contents

notes on archiving erasure

where does the story start?	3
creation	4
granny teaches her children how to eat poison	6
what I am afraid of	8
an incomplete legend on love	11
I write of my mother in the book of joy	12
great granny's last night	13
notes on archiving erasure	15
what love is	17
steps to safety	19
we thiefed our name	21

we find the fantastic

2 fat black women are making love	25
adventures of the third limb	26
granny speaks to the dead	28
the mermaid speaks	30
the ole higue goes hunting	32
moongazer	34
summoning the canaima	36
chickenfoot walks	38
chickenfoot meets god	39

chickenfoot loves	41
chickenfoot goes hunting with granny	42
chickenfoot laments	43
speculative fiction: apocalypse	44

american love

whoever died from a rough ride	47
An Ode to Rekia Boyd's Bloody Weave	49
if tamir rice and eric garner wore heels	50
unforgivable	52
Bresha Meadows Speaks on Divinity	53
the ballad of recy taylor	55
Nude Study of a Black Woman, 1850	57
good favor	59
lillian carter starts a letter to a former philandering lover	61
sovereign	62
harriet tubman is a lesbian	64
upon discovering that Daniel Holtzclaw's first accuser was a 57-year-old grandmother	65
when it is 2 pm in your office and you have a flashback to that moment you were raped	67
ritual	68
who we are human to	69
at the end	72

part 1.
notes on archiving erasure

where does the story start?

with outrageous grief
so luscious, so rare, we'll keep it for generations
bring it out at the finest of dinners, plant it in fields
and thresh its stalks at night.
it starts with a ring of jeweled mermaids beckoning
great uncle harold from solid ground to a golden city
submerged in shining black water,
his wife weeping and weeping at the shores among
his rough nets, harold's boat empty and rollicking
in the middle of a river. him rising after seven days
towards the pomeroon sun, pulled up wailing by scaled
lovely arms. it starts with the jumbee, dead slave children
hungry for friends, pining in the winds behind great granny's
house, drawn to salt and fevered blue fire. it starts
with broken glass, the surprise of blood
in a wife's waiting mouth, my great grandfather's hand
curled in a fist. it starts with a riot of stubborn love
more drunk than the pastor at my baptism, with one lie,
then another, then another, until a whole world is born
and we wait, a revolt of black girls.

creation

1. what you will leave behind

the beasts you carried on your back like horns   a patch-
    work of hazy legends that
can't bear fruit

2. the wedding night, 1958

you tell me about the lilies he brought you
dead from salt   the hours he spent
brushing your hair   how he kneeled
in front of you   cupped your trembling
face in his hands   as you wept

wishing you would die like the flowers

if his fingers would only grip harder   if your breathing
could only stop

but it is sinful to wish for death   and you
nearly died in the months before   five sisters
living off sick water and stale bread,   harvests
of cassava never reaped   the myth told is this

granddaddy saw you at 16   standing in kabakaburi
black hair swirled round your back   an ecstatic sigh
and fell in love

john smith had the same story.

3. the pomeroon

there is a hush born of dark cool moving waters   boats
that slice in and out   the sloth hanging deep 'neath

the trees   I know my chiny father   in dreams
he comes when the other men leave for work

    after mummy has gone out   hoe over back
    to dig in the garden   by our mothers' graves

    he will hold out his palm and beauty will just explode
    who else can do this sleight of hand

a fever of white birds flying over coca-cola water   congre-
gations of bamboo weaving out into a cathedral

lilies live in your hand

    you made me   you made me too

granny teaches her children how to eat poison

the lessons start in essequibo. the summer of 1965:
a crowded kitchen fat with pleading, another yellow gal,
20 with three children all hungry and wailing
mummy where daddy? 21 days spent restless waiting
and waiting by an unforgiving door and empty larder,
restless steel pots clanging on the stove
and it goes on like this: with a father shamed home after
three weeks of sweetness with another woman, back
to his own starving children nursed on boiled white rice
spiced with cassareep. his own belly big from love while
his wife spins time into fields of obeisance, all this love that
cannot be made into survival without him. three weeks of
hunger becomes *love*   the women he fucks   *ghosts*
and so on, until she can't eat without that lump in her throat
that makes her want to bawl out onto the street screaming
me husband don' wan' me
             me husband don' wan' me

watch her banging and banging these pots
cooking down truth into an inchoate stew

domesticate hurt into a monster we trust
more than our own eyes. help us still love
a congregation of men and the brute country
that made them until we while away whole life
times singing hymns that make us fat with belief
he doesn't beat me   it's the evil eye   why leave him

this litany sung as she watches the blossoming
bruise on my own mummy's arm
twenty years later while I play house at their feet,
set a plate brimming before her and say *eat*
meaning let your children live.

what I am afraid of

for Jacqueline Trimble

the mouse splayed on a glue trap
her gray body struggling for relief an

exhaust of dark shit breaking from her legs
wonder at how I dare to breach

the small lonely body contorted
and splayed in the kitchen.

how many others are there that chose
to leave her strayed on this trap?

did they see this baby
run and back away in faith?

nestle their bodies in warm quiet pipes
with new loves, fuck until another pup is born?

there are so many ways to come at peace with abandon.
the things we leave behind to save our own hide.

consider my father — illiterate in fidelity —
the brilliant long vine of women he courted.

I met one mistress at 8, beautiful, thick, insolent, saw
my father shaken, breath tight, lungs corseted by the ache.

he nursed a long drunken arc of desire in their arms.
my mother, his wife, frozen in an empty bed.

blocked calls unanswered.
pleasure she did not beget.

my mother only bothered to come alive to rear us
her arms rising in blessed parabola round her daughters

the extension cords she used to beat us, thickets
of welts on oiled chubby skin, our braided heads weaved

to her breast, my tears strangling her shirt, hot dinner,
then bed. her frantic bitter voice battling against

our sleep and father, him threatening to break her face.
I never saw him hit her. that tool they saved for us.

maybe that's why I beg partners to top me
flog my ass, fill me with cocks too wide, I know love

to be a wound that you pack and pack.

I am 35 and lonely.   I think of the lovers
left behind, abandoned on a trap.

still see the rose brown of ████'s
skin beneath my hands. the trembling house of

her breasts against my back. how she kissed
me when I cried at her inside, the bare

earned pulse of our quiet. how could she not
become my father, me my mother? us

strangling each other's necks on the floor
our children watching at bay, their soft brown

eyes steeled.

an incomplete legend on love

Mahaica, Guyana, 1935

at 10, granny jumped onto a grape tree, its boughs so fat
with fruit it diverted her eye from its own death. who could
blame her for climbing or the tree for falling, her right leg
smashed underneath its trunk. the blood spooling
like threads of saffron into the green fields the wound
a quake of splitting skin and bone in her thigh.
granny screaming into an open sky, until it birthed echoes
sending her brother winnie to find her from three miles away.
think on what it took to hear her call, what it means
for your heart to be so literate in your blood's
pain that you will run hours to save them a single ache.
we call this fealty. I call it prayer for the times we cannot
run to save each other, the little moments we horde
in tasks that separately would not be counted as holy

I write of my mother in the book of joy

most evenings find mummy pacing down cooling
paths in a blaze of blossoms. nothing that lived in
guyana can be nursed here, so instead her resistance
is found in the bud of hydrangeas, gladiolas, and a love
of hummingbirds. the most common of flowers
will be tended — during the summer she glories in the
rightness of blooming, dedicating hours to pulling
errant weeds that choke the root.

even in winter she is pledged to nursing life
in the bitterest of Maryland snow, think on the four lime trees
sheltering in our house, by the dining table, forcing
my blustering father to cower at least for a short while
in its branches, neighbors come by to exclaim
at the impossible orchard reared among wood-planked walls.

my mummy the stubborn farmer, laughing proudly
by its fruit. requests for advice returned with exacting
directions on wind, sun, and timing, yet when my sister
and I hear her, what we think of are two little girls
reared less gently than this — her a young lonely mother
with sometimes brutal hands, but here I am
crying at the lesson of her bowed back in the garden,
hands dug into a mire of dirt, stubbornly
willing love into life.

great granny's last night

beyond her window, she can hear the strains
men leaving the fields, singing in anticipation of another
night sweet with food and women, their faces tender
with sweat, ringed in mud
hands gripping machetes, blades slung
upwards towards a dimming sun

her pipe lays packed and unsmoked by her bed,
clean sheets huddled round her, cups of
milky tea and weeping held quiet in the next room

granny will tell me all she saw that night,
death — a great horned thing
sitting side by side with god in one small
cramped room by a huge dark river. the birds
cawing in blue ecstasy, elvis's love me tender played
on repeat until even the record player begs for relief,
the pick worn down with playing lyrics so
tired they can't help but be real,

elvis in a glittery jumpsuit and heels wailing
for my darlin I love you

and when he hits that high note, pulls away
the mic, crooning *love me true* even
death and god dance together,

weep in each other's embrace, smiling
for an old woman losing breath as the
time bears down

she says *I just need him to forgive one
last thing* made her body a confession

hands stretched out in the air towards
a white white road filled with flowers, fruit, and light,
no work or babies to deliver just liming and a
shining laughing death
ready to deliver her, a squalling wrinkly child

notes on archiving erasure

love does not begin and end the way we seem to think it does. love is a battle, love is a war; love is a growing up.

—James Baldwin

when I say
I love my family
what I mean
is I worship
the battle. you
can't wish away
creation or reorder
blood. childishly
I thought we could
retell story(ies)
I mean to say,
I can't lie. in truth
there are wretched
days I call my sister
and ask *was this
real? did this happen?*
she says nothing
part of love can be
called refusing to
answer. my mother
says *let things lie*
she means murder it
let our shame be

a suffocating vine:
we were made to
believe that everything
we bore was ugly: a family
of shell-shocked
gods fleeing
their own clay — yet,
I will come back to
the door of our own home
sit at its steps, and fall in
love with the slow order
of our creation, the seasons
it took to urge kindness into
our natures. how we won
glory even as the city fell.

what love is

after Phillip Levine

you are 8, holding hands with
your little sister in the back of your father's car,
watching as he slows the engine down to a
bare murmur and pleads with your mother
marching down the highway, the flowers
on her hat trembling like her hands as
she walks away from her husband
as if she could walk away from this life
and all she borrowed to buy it.
you will focus on your father's pleadings
the empty promises to treat her kindly,
stop sleeping with other women, and
your sister will start to wail asking
is mummy not coming back home
no one has the breath to answer her,
least of all you. in your baby wisdom,
all you can do is wish beyond heaven
that she won't listen to daddy's lies
keep marching away from that car
and be happy without you
you'll look at the dead
buck on the side of the road, next to
your mother, as she stops to listen
to your father's lies, the deer's neck

smashed, his body still
beautiful, the fur soft, flesh ripped
exposing a dark black machine
so soft, stinking, and fragile that years
later you'll remember the risk of loving
something that wild. what it gave up
to run across that road, the sheer
dumb luck it held for the thousands
of days it ran riot over a shrinking
forest, and the men determined to kill
it, halve its neck, and embrace the head
as a trophy. one day, you'll be brave
and ask your mother why she stayed
why she kept her children and raised
them with a man who thought taming
was an act of tenderness. you won't
listen to the answer

steps to safety

1. listen to luther nonstop
2. wear low-cut shirts
3. quit your job by staging a praise dance version of beyonce's "freedom" in front of your racist-ass boss. get the cashier at seven 11 to do kendrick lamar's verse
4. call your granny, cry
5. cry again with your daddy
6. end the call when he asks about your 401k
7. think about the positives about the trump administration — namely pence's hair, how does a white man get his hair so on fleek? does he use blue magic? does he have a black barber? is his name lamont? is lamont a republican? did lamont give pence a do-rag? does pence wear the do-rag during black history month?
8. call your granny again, discuss pence's hair, compare it with bernie's at the DNC. listen to her hushed whispers in the bathroom when she shares that bernie could get it
9. weep again in your white therapist's office
10. listen as your white therapist says, *I don't really think trump will round up all black LGBTQ people*
11. wonder how she quantifies *all.* would all include everybody except lamont? pence's lover? who are the exclusions?

19

12. realize you are weary of white disbelief
13. look at her face while you are crying. see her eyes water. they are probably allergies
14. read of the 8 trans people who have committed suicide since the elections
15. think of pence again and all the black and queer blood on his hands, trump's silly wig and the million dollars he has invested in the pipeline
16. read *macbeth*. imagine trump in tights and a codpiece. sage your eyes
17. text back and forth with blair about countries to move to. think of how blackness is a gamble wherever you go
18. when you think of home, you think of granny, a 90-year-old woman, a living altar rooted here
19. ask your heart if it can flee
20. listen to the answer

we thiefed our name

translate this into any tongue
and you will have a story
of white smooth-skinned evangels
with hot palms and unnamed dark
women ready to fuck in the embrace
of open fields. one uncle tells us
of free black men running past
the threat of trinidad into
guyana, another of corsica
still more speak of ships, another
a big rambling house more confused
than its yellow children. in truth
everyone is clumsy with our blood
our family tree proves it:
look for a root and sap comes wandering in
none of us will ever know our mothers
just burst forward from job's great black head
colossal, lying, and feasting.

part 2
we find the fantastic

2 fat black women are making love

and the joke is right there, ready, shuddering
and alive — rife with promise. there are so many
paths that have been out-worn out for a quick
easy laugh: tyler perry strutting with a gun and wig,
screaming rotund and loud like a madea would,
martin calling out *yo mama* on television, or the
meme of a young woman shot underhand
her belly in love with a tight skirt, hands moving
towards an open mouth, look at everything she devours
imagine it: does it make you hungry too?

2 fat black women are making love, on a bed, on the
floor, and they are weeping for joy — they are crying
great folds of flesh flushing and shaking, one cannot
look in the mirror save for thinking of her daddy —
all this ugly and skin together, counts the men who
say they hate her body as they do bitter cops and
dead black boys.

2 fat black women are making love — and they touch
each other like they can hold it. honeyed, profane, bawdy —
like patriots, like their bodies have never been folded
into freezers, screamed at on streets, coaxed, or threatened
sweet, like they have names, like we will know them.

adventures of the third limb

I want to name our cock chocolate thunder, tammy thinks
I have lost my mind. I see our cock as a blaxploitation
heroine resplendent in the finest of neon spandex, draped in
golden chains and a velvet cape, stiff in resolution to kick
any jive turkey punk muthafucka ass into submission.

our cock has framed pictures of prince on the wall,
and listens to deon estus to show her sensitive side.

she is fluent in seven languages, drinks dos equis, can
paint, sing gospel, praise dance and is head usher
at the church of dynamic discipleship. our cock
is the renaissance dick, and if you are looking at
her sideways: bitch, what has your cock done for you lately?

our cock doesn't hide when company comes, stalks out
butt naked in sequined pumps, shining with lube,
sits spread-eagled on the dinner table and says
embarrassing shit about things she
would do to kerry washington.

and when everyone else leaves, and only the three of us
are left, all limbs and laughter, she pulls me and tammy closer,
our pussies climbing up her veined girth. this is how we fit together
loud, tight, and eager, our wails her composition, agitated
aching notes — accesso and broken chord.

in the studio later with smokey, outfitted in a double-
breasted stacey adams suit, matching gators, pinky ring, and straw
panama hat, she'll share a blunt, then play *cruising*
while talking shit about how hard we came, and the scent
of wet — but in that moment

        oh!   my love!

granny speaks to the dead
Kabakaburi, Guyana, January 2018

the wind is sulk
and salt, shaking
bamboo arched into
a green prayer for our path.
granny leads the way
mummy beside her, walking
to the cluster of nameless
concrete graves that
compose the only family
history we know.
everything before 1913
is a fruitless game
of imagination made
for nights at home after rum
and black cake
granny and her sisters
arguing over who died
first and how:
aunt rosamund, baker
of the sweetest cakes
in adventure, lost
to her own love
of sugar, or uncle clive
a dainty black man

with sooty skin
softer than the river
he walked into, beguiled
by the call of mermaids
or drink.
even granny's history
is a twist
of ready evasion:
a young girl, eldest
of thirteen, who lived
hungry, breathless, and
beautiful, until my grandfather
found her on the waters
of demerara, took her
home and said
you are mine.

now, fifty years later
granny is back home
beside me
on hands and knees
cleaning a baby's grave
talking to her of death
saying *my sweet gal*
I'm here, keep me company
in my dreams, nuh?
I've learned from her how
to make your own story:
just let the dead in

the mermaid speaks*

everything they have said is true
I have eaten men as you would a tangerine
thoughtlessly   reverently

juice smeared about my mouth

perhaps you would blame me   call me bloodthirsty
along with the rest of my kin   the canaima
the ole higue   even the mazaruni   roust up a gang
of the young brave on palm wine to come and stake me
and I laugh as surely as you weep on my shores
(this ownership you'll forgive me
I took it as the dutch did your children)

your forebears came on the same
hunt after I ate another man   (your granddaddy?)
forgive me   he was lovely
ripe copper skin warmed
with the sun   singing among the white lotus
as if he could charm the roots of trees   into fealty

---

*In Guyana, mermaids, also known as water babies, have a long and complex history within historical narratives exploring the enslavement of African people. Sometimes seen as harbingers of good luck, mermaids were also warned to be cursed creatures who would kidnap your beloved and drive them mad.

I remember weeping
with my sisters below in our city
maybe he wept too
it's been so long I can't be sure
and there is nothing
I want to pretend with you
 so I did what was impossible
swam up   struggling past the pleas of my own mother
 burst through the pomeroon and beseeched
him into my arms   (yes I say begged without shame
you know the men of your blood
 what they can drive you to do)

and forward he came
fearful of drowning dancing into my naked red arms
          and when I ate him   he urged me on
sang with delight as my teeth met
the cradle of his flesh   I have heard his wife crying
at our shores   hands tethered to her children
dragging them to and fro
as if her love could raise him
the fishermen say she
went mad with grieving
is this true?

the ole higue goes hunting*

legend holds that I am
ugly and stooped, covered in frightful
disdain. I glory in my own
sight: naked black wrinkled flesh, breasts
low-hanging ripe fruit, my
sex a shining damp shell.

at night while you slumber
I go flying crowned
in blue fire above the mahaica,
my skin left sleeping in bed.

there are those who would
argue my midnight visits spur madness
report of women who cup machetes as
they would my breasts and do a violence
to their men. I say the taste of me
intoxicates, bewitches my beloveds
to cut what keeps them tethered
and sighing, toiling in heat for a

The ole higue is a myth created by Dutch enslavers in Guyana. A hunchbacked old woman, the ole higue was said to depart her skin at night and beguile young women into killing their families.

man that does little good. in truth
this way is no easier: boys
spread white salt and rice in
strict lines to bar me from my own skin
my own beloveds shy with fear
when they first see me
but then I reach out my hand, hold
them to my chest and sing the history
of old black women digging and crafting
this ancient earth into consciousness. I say
this is yours, take it, and they come
shuddering with power

moongazer[*]

> *I will not ask you where you came from*
> *I will not ask it,*
> *neither should you*
> —Hozier

let me say this: I was human once
and so frail, the weight of a machete
could split my back working in these fields
we harvested cane all throughout the day
longing for the call of night, the
cool black hollow it would bring even now
I remember my woman — mighty as she was

crying after a day's work, my own
hands trembling as we suckled stolen cane
together, that sugar the only thing that
cared if we lived or died. I buried her
in those same fields we slaved, then swooned
blindly into the sweet of a velvet dark
kept hearing my love
calling me deeper still. I grew wild
in my grief, dreamt her a moon
reaching down, until finally I grew taller
to meet her voice, a giant mighty as her

---

[*] *The moongazer is a bloodthirsty monster fabled to hunt those who come into the fields at night. The Dutch created the moongazer to stop slaves from stealing sugarcane after dark.*

oh, my god, what stories these white
men will tell! let them say I would
kill my own blood rather than let
them eat, stalk sugarcane fields
as I would my own heart. you
know me, what I have done
to find my darling: look at her
crowned by nothing but the stars
in this bowl of sky. her dark hands lifted
soft and worn, my gaze
a patient delight. look at her
there beyond the moon
singing to an entranced black tide
look at me, forever in thrall, slave
to no one but wonder

summoning the canaima*

I feel the breath of the wolf in my ear
at night I close my eyes
dream of what you will kill
the white crane, its neck barely torn
or perhaps my master, his tongue splayed
across that thin angry sneer
will you bring it to me? this unbearable
gorgeous prey, dragged bedside
bloodless and still

I could lose my soul for conjuring
evil like I have the right to call god
and demand an answer, I could
lose my man for what I've done
strung up on some tree as penance
for bedding a witch
his back flayed with a whip
in thrall with the secrets of his flesh
I could cause my child's head
to be dashed out on the stones
that stops the essequibo from flooding
this white man's plantation

---

* The canaima is a mythological creature conjured by people to wreak revenge on those who have harmed them.

placed by black
hands spilling black blood
I could lose my life for this, cause
my aunties to throw threadbare aprons
over their blessed heads and cry out for air

yet still, I want to open my ribs
take my ache
mold it like clay   into death
a sickle to drive my enemies into
something past madness

give me a reason to leave them alone
arrest this sorrow inside me   sealed
like I don't know what's nesting inside

chickenfoot walks

the way you think a man with a machete in his
6 passenger van should — all sinew and black amble
his women are a tribe of big dark angels in tight dresses with
breasts like freshly buttered bakes, cook up falls in
love at least twice a week and he drives them mad
with his stories of the jumbees he's fought off in the
interior, his hands roving a velvet spell against their hair.
women, they come look for he at the drink shop all hours of
the day, darla and suzanne fought over him — chickenfoot
grinning like a mad king in the corner, in a tore-up white shirt
and bare pants, eating prawns and chow mein, while pretty
darla wept *why yuh keepin anudda woman so*, suzanne
creeping up behind her with a rock and knocked darla so
hard upside the head, the skull split like meat, and
darla keeps crawling wailing *i'll giv' yuh my blood* till
chickenfoot leaves with suzanne only to steal away again
during the early morning chorus of toads. darla's mummy
thinks suzanne set an evil eye on her, darla can't stop
weeping, just dreams of cook up and his knives
inside her, cutting, cutting, until he loves

chickenfoot meets god

and she is a big
big black woman
thick thigh meat all dark
knotted hair, lips a smashed
ripe heart, soft and trembling
even when she smiles
her gap teeth bright, shining
the whistle of air when she
laughs a siren call to chickenfoot
that he can't forget, spends
hours trying to summon
like a magician

sometimes he love she
too much, bangs
on every door, window
and wall in her blessed
house till he breaks
in. swears off the rum
shop, then whirls
round her kitchen till a feast
erupts, prays at her feet
for grace, then pulls god in closer
whispers *who else yuh love*
but me enters in
between her legs and feasts
for days. god
drunk in his frenzy

then there are months
where he forgets her, chases
after other fine women
and drink, she lays in a
locked closet weeping
into her sister's shoulder
holding her arms, god's bare
skin shining a bruised plum

chickenfoot loves
at age thirteen

his mummy, her face a waxing yellow moon, the chin
a dark field curled and twisted. every sunday
chickenfoot tends this garden with her, tweezers in hand
a slight silver mirror grasped in her palm the color
of ripe plantains hissing in a pan. each follicle loosed
from her flesh more stubborn than the next, black hair
encased in a bulb of white. chickenfoot loves her beard
and the flesh that rears it even when she weeps declares
herself *too ugly* to go to church and even look at god
curses her stubborn blood that makes new things
grow even when she has killed it with her own hands.
chickenfoot loves reginald from section k
their lips firm against each other in the one shadow
old lady wong's house provided. the pleasure
their tongues reared in each other. chickenfoot loves
reginald even more when he and
a gang of boys beat him for walking too sweet to the
cricket field. the calls of *faggot* bleeding
through the air, chickenfoot's fists joining with reginald's
chest again and again. how reginald kept rising to his feet
stubborn and bold, till the boys left him be, and chickenfoot
leads him home, sat reginald down in his own bedroom
and wept before him, *why ah hurt yuh?* their hands
growing into each other, rushing to close the wound.

chickenfoot goes hunting with granny

age six

loud nights in the interior, the blade
foreign in his baby palm, granny's knife
strapped between her soft dark breasts,
a machete trailed back in war
with one silver and black braid, that her man
Shakespeare will unbraid every evening
and weep *so sweet so sweet*. Shakespeare hunts granny
like the meat they catch, he wants her black and trembling,
trapped *a ghost an angel a bitch fuckin' cunt.*
chickenfoot wants her too,
promises granny big big golden houses
where blood stays in the body, draws pictures
of her laughing like a spell. how granny weeps
at the river, chickenfoot's baby arms
round her neck, his hand a waiting fist.

chickenfoot laments

begins to cry at the bar,
tears falling onto the crisp linen suit
darla takes him home
a blooming house all lace and pink bougainvillea,
serves curried lizard sweet and ripe on flowered plates, she
smiling and smiling as chickenfoot drinks more spiced rum, talks
so about his granny and her knives, the one room and bed
they slept in at the corner of a big dark water, how he
could press against her when the cock crowed and
she smelled of tea and night. the men she loved who
beat her   left the cupboards bare

chickenfoot takes darla to her white bed, and eats
her for hours, holds her like he would his granny
arms curled round her form like a shield
weeps as night falls for how her heart will break
when he leaves her, weeps for the man he adores
and could never touch like this, weeps for
the warm cradle of darren's skin, knowing he would bury
a machete like love into his belly, if darren ever
dared to call out to him on a crowded street
darla's bed nothing but a river for his ache

speculative fiction: apocalypse

let's say the world doesn't end
and you go to its edge
and yes, it is a real place
the ocean pounding at the gates   white foam
winged and salty and lonely sluicing
and feral   will you
stay there, on your hands and knees
looking for god   count your infinite
offenses into an unending rosary try to be good
on a land you never really
could claim kin to   tilling your
lonely into a field

or will you find another way
make your own heaven   know
the seed that makes you   roam
this world like tina turner in mad max
black bad assed   and platinum haired
enthroned in your own bare skin   beguiled in
your own story   its siren call

part 3
american love

whoever died from a rough ride

for freddie gray

I love Baltimore because I love blackness:
kneeling before a black woman while
she runs hands sweating with grease and heat
over my head, my scalp a swoon of submission
I first learned touch here, caught
between the walls of my mother's legs on Sundays
a purple fine-tooth comb parting maps in the lovely
rough mess of my hair perfumed
by grass and sweat from hours spent
idling in dusk with my sister, holding hands
as we witnessed the daily fall of the sun's reign.

I love blackness because I love touch:
in Baltimore touch is a reverence, how a man I barely
know sees me weeping, places a palm on my shoulder
asking nothing but *baby you good? you good?*
feeling everything like a hymn
a whole black stubborn city quaking in grief
planted on a harbor feeding off sick water and lead
and still its streets hum with joy
arabbers placing two hands on a watermelon
closing their eyes to divine its sweetness, the brother
who rides on horseback during pride, galloping

through Charles Street, a jeweled shine of sweat
yes, Baltimore knows something about beauty
how it's found in the resistance of state
the memory of breath, yes
it's there, in our hands, the magic
of a little girl's braid dancing double
dutch in front of brooding cops, the falling
houses behind her, it's bones
chanting *we won't leave we won't leave*

An Ode to Rekia Boyd's Bloody Weave*

you, a worn note of sugar burnt white want
the weft of hair left unbloodied and blacker than sky,
I can dream the scissors that cut into you, the hands that
grasped your scalp, as follicles sang out the intent of one
bullet as it forged straight into your sweet, sweet skull,
past the muscle of brain and caused the very life
of you to seize up, your blank eyes a requiem
to unthought kisses, the rough pad of feet down
steps in mornings, the very cups of brewed coffee
that will grow cold without you

oh my dear heart, they cut so many of our dead women
into pieces, they will not grieve your hair.

---

* *After the conclusion of the trial of the officer who had killed Rekia Boyd, the Chicago Police Department mailed back Rekia Boyd's effects to her family. Among her belongings was a Ziploc bag filled with Rekia Boyd's hair.*

if tamir rice and eric garner wore heels

we'd drive by their dead bodies,
find some other right man to mourn
no houses would burn down
news film would crumble to dust
and their brothers would cry in shame

we'd lay them out in suits instead of dresses,
call them by their birth names
and when the bodies come to the mortician
carrion dragged from the side of the road,
limbs splayed, organs blue cold,
he'll close the eyes clouded with more terror
then there are trees in chibok
267 black girls struck mute into knowing/drowned in Allah

we'd forget wasilat, a 14-year-old nigerian wife
preparing dinner for umar, her fat husband
destruction is a sloppy cook,
slight hands sow meat with rat poison
— what hours did she spend alone with him,
laid astride him
till he called out something so hard in her, blood shattered.
in court, her father will recall between tears that she never
    wanted to marry him

4 people died from the meat she served that night.
I wonder if she sat amidst those bodies at the warped
    dinner table and bitter red heat
head high,
hair falling,
a queen,
and let out a wail as mighty as any man

howl like a wounded dog, riots of wind and fire, burn
your own fucking house down, forget sakia and britney,
stand like an idiot cut, bloody and bruised before god in a
bombed-out theater and answer why we'll pour out onto
the street like bright red river for a sweet boy, but never in
the light of day remember to march once for a black queer
girl doused in gasoline and set on fire
screaming for her loves   a million flames

unforgivable

every time I wake up, I want it to be a nightmare —LaPorsha Washington*

is the stubborn sun
faithless
in its bald grieving.
so much is ugly
the memories
of your daughter
fallow blood rising from
her. it is unforgivable
that you'll learn to live
this turn of the earth
without her, that death
is blessed with
her name.

---

* *LaPorsha Washington is the mother of Jazmine Barnes, a seven-year-old girl shot and killed while riding in a car with family members.*

Bresha Meadows Speaks on Divinity*

god is a black girl
who once had to kill her own father.
say the social workers listened with kind
white eyes as she wept, her bare skin
a constellation of ripening bruises. say
god shuddered on walks home. ran away
fifteen times before she was 13, sat in
tight airless rooms hustled up in sleep clothes
and stank breath, repeated
her rosary *he beats us he beats*
us he beats us he beats he beats he beats
how the counselors shook their heads, asked
questions like *does he hit you with an open*
or closed hand, buttoned their good
woolen coats in the blind ohio winter and
took her back home. when god comes to school
wailing breaking chairs screaming
he will kill me
a chorus of white women hover round her
confused lovely angels, pronouncing
her name a supplication.

---

* *Bresha Meadows is a fourteen-year-old Black girl convicted of killing her abusive father in self-defense.*

god cut herself to
remember or forget how history changes
he will kill me to *are you sure.* how
she dreamt at night of trees and running
her mother's head
cleft into galaxies of blood
her father's hands thick dark laughing
rocks carving their flesh
her mother begging her not to tell, says
he will kill me and god can't stop
imagining the sweet jump of a trigger.
god cried over her father
sleeping, gun in hand, how
the bullets exited the chamber, how
he died saying her name, god
bloody and keening on the floor, her mother
screaming a break knitted
into the end of a heartbeat. god's arms
around her father. god is a black
girl in love with living, a sacrament on how to be
disbelieved, forgotten and
rise a thousand times over

the ballad of recy taylor*

Abbeville, Alabama

act just like you do with your husband or I'll cut your damn throat
—Herbert Lovett

to be an american is to love
roads that tried to kill
me, dust, the desperate
beat of fannie's
stout white fists against that green
chevy, a murder
of white men packed inside, their
pale hands a lesson on patriotism and
allegiance. to be an american
is to love god, to love how
we can call out his name
maybe a thousand times in one
endless bloody breaking night, to glory
in the silence of an answer
that never comes.

---

* *Recy Taylor was a Black woman kidnapped and gang-raped by seven white men on September 3, 1944. She pressed charges, aided by Rosa Parks, and eventually brought her assailants to trial.*

I am an american
because I call a thing
a thing: love
is my child, home
is wherever my daddy
goes: frantic searching
for my body
and what those seven
white men did
in all those godless hours
was rape me
laugh   train steel at my heart

my god, if I waited
for you, maybe I'd be dead
in that lonesome forest, my bare
breasts holding a grove
of pecan trees, the taste
of my blood lingering
in its fruit, a shamed
footnote in another black man's
sorrow. you let me keep
my tongue, I'll use it to set
this road afire

Nude Study of a Black Woman, 1850

J. Paul Getty Museum, Artist Unknown

to you, I am worth less than
the camera you shot me with
the money you make selling
this daguerreotype to other
white men who hide me
from their wives in leather trunks
fraught with the smoke of cigars
who knew that a hundred years
later america would break its bank
for me, fiending
for an image that contracts upon
view. after this pose, where
I recline on your wife's finest
silk chaise, and urge my fingers
into the very quick of me
I will hurry on my rough cotton
and go down to the kitchen
leave my hands unwashed
to bake your honeyed biscuits
rounded in the heart of my palm
and serve them before you
my good master, my iron
and labor weeping from your

pores. d'you smell me sir?
my pleasure? my ache?
tell me again who you
think I am

good favor
after great great granny's photograph

like any good higue, I was beautiful
once: this picture is proof enough
of blood, proof that something
nameless can and will haunt you
how one generation's griefs
can abide for a thousand more
my own daughter could not
speak of me for the century
of her life without tears
that water blessed me
as did her silence
your mother would
tell you *don't ask great granny*
about her mummy and so you
obeyed, just sucked back
words into your throat
where everything beautiful
and grieving can be caught.
this kind of quiet is an impossible
love. black folks don't get
to own their bodies, why
should their names
be different? I was murdered
by my husband's hand

and now even in death
you let him get the last word.
my picture is
a talisman perched
in every last one
of my grandchildren's
homes. me bonnetted
and severe in stiff colorless
splendor: let this picture
be a lesson, the yeast
that finally makes you rise up
against any fool who tries
to say they know you how
you lived because they
believe they know
how you died
the picture shows
you nothing but a docile, solemn
yellow girl, her lungs starved
and gasping above a
cage of whalebone.

you'll never see
me, for all you could have
known, my legs were a coiled scaled fin
glittering, green, majestic
my chest a feathered round of fire
fecund and gleaming.
what does it matter?
just live, let me find
who I am

lillian carter starts a letter to a former philandering lover

for great granny
London, 1963

                my dear, mr. chin
it could be supposed any sensible woman would stay   a man cheats as quick as they breathe
here, a big egg-yellow gal with scant hair in thrall   lovesick, I was a machine for your punishment
forced, I see it now, sir —   and yes, those nights we spent roving in bed
the Guyana dark calling and calling so sweet   the pastor your chest, my thighs the choir
      two great fat bodies collided with the force of desire
if, pushed to confess, I loved it when you reared up   in pleasure and screamed *glory glory*
after a lifetime of angry brutish men. I found you   a sort of black paradise
  I prepared a daily feast of hallelujahs to lay at your feet, I a panting forest as you ate
hear me cry so lonesome and wild to this white man's god for a little plot of half pleasure
                thank you jesus, thank you!

sovereign

I am not in love, but I am open to persuasion
— Joan Armatrading

I am 20
the first time I learn
how to persuade
my own body
my hands rocking
plaintively against my clitoris
past buds of curled hair sprung
in witness
to pleasure
those long afternoons spooled
like a ribbon of ache: pliant,
bright   incoherent

I am 34   the first time I divine
a flood between my thighs
screaming *jesus*
dazzled by my own making
how   gorgeous   how
lovely to rule   hold dominion
over a universe   reap
its harvest   ready
and blooming

I tell you, I worship
at the curve of my breast, feed on it
as you would bread
and meat

I tell you, I have fed myself a thousand times
and come back calling my name
in a state of joy — wild, spinning, and ready

harriet tubman is a lesbian

remember the time I said harriet tubman was a lesbian, and laughed straight for fifteen minutes? jabari said *fuck that, harriet wasn't trying turn the underground into henrietta's.* but shit, I need a hero, a full on black queer woman setting fire to slave ships, cursing out white motherfuckers and going home to love on phyllis hyman's fine assed great great granny. I want a history where harriet and sojourner get together and make that cataclysmic, head banging *good god* kind of love while luther serenades them, with skin so shining it looks like he just swam all up in johnsons and johnsons. I want him there singing to them, his sequined blazer the north star they follow hand in hand under the cover of knotted trees and vines that rise up to hide them. the glow of lightning bugs, grasshoppers humming as luther executes a smooth two step to *wait for love* — prince behind him humping the stage. oh! and that moment when sojourner bends down, cups her hands, dips them into a running creek, and says, *c'mon harriet, drink*, watches the soft pulse and bend of her woman's neck as she feeds sweet water from her palm — and she thinks *someday I'll make me a poem about how I love her.* that night the first time they found the salt to kiss, while luther reapplies his eyeliner, and prince takes over the mic crooning *baby baby baby what's it going to be tonight*, sojourner and harriet latching onto each other's bodies, sucking nipples like they deliver honeyed wine, hollering a blue joyful streak over and over in an answering chorus

upon discovering that Daniel Holtzclaw's first accuser was a 57-year-old grandmother*

Oklahoma City, Oklahoma

I thought, my god, he is going to kill me
—Survivor Testimony

I think of the kiss of the cutlass against stalks of sugarcane,
black sweaty arms swinging, dark hands tending to white
necks and pots of plain food. think of the lullabies
of the pomeroon, long-limbed stories of slave uprisings,
fifteen thousand strong, knives sunk into the hearts of
masters, blushing of blood onto the wet banks
of the demerara the slaves that marooned there:
great big beautiful black women
with hard stomachs and pipes chock full of tobacco.
no one knows how many men died here. the bloodletting
turning rivers pitch black. white men buried at night
by the shore — oh! and the gardens they grew in their graves:

---

* *Daniel Holtzclaw is a former police officer who was convicted on eighteen counts of forcible rape. It is reported that he assaulted hundreds of Black poor women in Oklahoma City during his time on the force.*

roots of calalloo, cassava, and yams cleaved
to bones of jumbees — demons can't kill you if
you make them feed you.

they made a feast of organs, turned into mangroves
nursed out sweet-baked pone, curried laba, daal, and
pepperpot. my great granny had her own garden
amidst graves, tilled soil until whole generations fed
off stewed riots and grief, wiped their mouths
and called it sweet. think of the grannies who wrestle
their demons every day, and usher it onto a
plate a slave master's head seasoned with brutal economy.

imagine the armies of grannies behind daniel holtzclaw's
accuser their sacred breath on her shoulders as she spells
out cold black words strong as divinity *you tried to kill me
you should've tried harder*

when it is 2 pm in your office and you have a flashback to that moment you were raped

Baltimore, November 2017

go into the bathroom, make an animal of your lips.
snarl, push your back against the wall, be grateful for everything your body forgot, make your story the anchor: *I was only six* see her on the floor: that big moon-faced semicolon of boy trying to stuff all his human into her. imagine all the questions you could ask if he showed up today all lost and foolish in those dirty white sneakers he dragged every day in the new jersey dirt searching for mica, like was it true that his daddy would make the brothers strip before he beat them
— the skin peeling like bark, how you marveled the way black could go from walnut to white, the blush of red inside   saida, would you kill him? for these thirty years of loss copulating — all this time you been here so black and woman waiting to be believed? or would you know that this lesson would've come some other way, as sure as the moon. you are weeping for the days you would gladly bury every knife in his chest, let agony's children sing an anthem to his bones. imagine the feast you would have before his body your hands   now grown   closed round his throat once again, his eyes a forest primeval could you love him then? that fourteen-year-old bruised boy in a torn hoodie immolating whole cities — would you love the american in him?

ritual

I never knew what it took to die
if no one closes your lids, your
eyes are scotch taped closed
if your mouth is left open, someone
will come and break your jaw put
your body back together so that
your family can come and see something
they know. the white hot violence it
takes to break your body into something
familiar hide the bed sores hide the shit
anything to pretend the work of dying
never existed shuffled off into a patchwork
of bodies twisted broken and turned into
the humans we wanted them to be. maybe
that's why no one says much
when bodies of trans women are found
carved all over dark cities chopped into
arms legs and limbs that can't be made
whole or familiar, but instead strange
leaving only teeth to identify whole
lives by, picking out fillings and extractions
to separate their blood from others
how did they say goodbye? what is
left to bring back home to a cemetery
or resting place — who can close their eyes
hold the body and remember what is familiar
in battle

who we are human to

my best friend is worried enough
about me that he has bought me a purse.

when I can stop weeping,
I look at the picture tiger texted me of it —
the shining pink leather and woven fabric,
think of the time he took to pick it out,
his child dancing to salsa on his lap
while a few blocks down
men in dark uniforms
come again for another family —
hustled behind a locked door
and I dream of plantations:
the lonely bitter wood of slave cabins.

I am watching unremarkable men on television
wonder how foreign they would find my grief.
a calf keening over a slaughtered mother

flint hasn't had water in over a thousand days,
sandra is dead, and
my heart feels like a mule.

I've been thinking since then
of all the people who have put their hands
on my body.

the man
who raped
me at 6

how I bolted
a wounded deer
my barrettes clacking
against the tiled bathroom floor
his hands on the lock, my heart
closing and opening, a fearful fist

my first girlfriend arching
a butcher knife against
my chest

mummy says
it was god that stopped her from

plunging that steel
into my heart, my
friends tell me not to think on it,

twelve years later, I can't help but marvel at
the miracle of her pause
cold blade in hand,
drunk on who she could end,
looked at my throat
and felt the breath caught inside

tiger has never found my grief foreign —
if he did, he has kept it to himself.
I remember the time he bent between
my legs, and as
gently as any lover searched
my cleft for the stuck tampon
I had left behind. how
he called my name *saida* like
sister while pulling
the bloody cotton
trapped inside
never backed away
at the explosion of rusted
red growth that bloomed out
but laughed at the rancid smell
of what grows inside you when
decay is forced in.

this is the most wonderful grace I can find:

we are nothing if not houses to each other that can hold
all sorts of brutal tender memory, make rooms of flesh
and light where we bear witness to the most horrible
rock each other in our arms and whisper y*es yes*
I know

at the end

is a 102-year-old woman more yellow then candied ginger,
peppery cuss and purple hibiscus drowning in a sea
of wrinkles. ten days ago she upped and called
her granddaughter, said she was tired of living, and
stopped eating. took to her bed, a triumphant queen
enthroned in a rich asylum of ironed sheets redolent
in the mist of vanilla and salt, dreamt of boats clanging
in Barbados, the days her swollen legs could run
by her son near the shore, how the brown sweating men
would put down their nets just to watch them dance,
nearly cut their fingers gutting the rainbow of wahoo fish,
granddaddy lost in the crook of her arm, his little knee
socks dirty with gold sand she'd wash later in the weep
of wax candles, the room filled with the soft flush
of his funky little boy breath, a hungry icebox
and a fevered fry pan that never cooked a meal
for anyone but her child. great granny fed herself on love.
why should she die any different?

Acknowledgments

I am thankful to these journals, anthologies, and websites for publishing the following work:

"I write of my mother in the book of joy," *About Place*

"granny teaches her children how to eat poison," "what love is," "we thiefed our name," and "good favor," *Arlington Journal*

"the ballad of recy taylor" and "the ole higue goes hunting," *Auburn Avenue*

"Nude Study of a Black Woman, 1850," "lillian carter starts a letter to a former philandering lover," "sovereign," "speculative fiction: apocalypse," and "the mermaid speaks," *Barrelhouse*

"creation," *Beltway Poetry Quarterly*

"adventures of the third limb," *Delaware Poetry Review*

Previous versions of "chickenfoot walks," "chickenfoot loves," "chickenfoot goes hunting with granny," "when it is 2 pm in your office and you have a flashback to that moment you were raped," and "who we are human to," *Drunk in the Midnight Choir*

"summoning the canaima," *A Gathering of Tribes*

"where does the story start?," *HEart Online*

"notes on archiving erasure," *Hobart Pulp*

"great granny's last night" and "steps to safety," *Not Without Our Laughter: Poems of Humor, Sexuality & Joy*

"Bresha Meadows Speaks on Divinity," *Origins Journal*

"if tamir rice and eric garner wore heels," *Pluck! The Affrilachian Journal of Arts and Culture*

A previous version of "chickenfoot laments," *Plume*

"2 fat black women are making love" and "harriet tubman is a lesbian," *Split This Rock*

"ode to Rekia Boyd's bloody weave," *Torch Literary Arts*

"granny speaks to the dead" and "moongazer," *West Trestle Review*

Gratitude

Deep, heartfelt thanks to the Cave Canem Foundation, the Rubys Artist Grants, Blue Mountain Center, and the Watering Hole for creating magical spaces to write, love, and be.

To the Black Ladies Brunch Collective (Teri, Tafisha, Niki, Celeste, Katy, Anya) and the Rooted Collective (Blair, Kalima, Nkiru, Malik Ti, Alexis), my deepest love.

To my wife, Renee Agostini Bostic, you are infinitely patient, wise, and big-hearted. I am so lucky.

To my parents, Michael and Anne, and little sister Anika — I love you deeply.

To my teachers, Omari Daniel, Phyllis Viccellio, Jan Beatty, Toi Derricote. Thank you for seeing me, for reading my work, and saying *yes, keep writing*.

To all those who aided my research in Guyana, including Great Aunt Ruby, Ole Man Pappy, and Joan Cambridge.

To all who read previous drafts for their support, care, and vision, including Tara Betts, Lisbeth White, Lyrae Van Clief Stefanon, and so many others.

To my best friends, Bobby Bannister, Samantha Lea, Adey Dimalanta, Akara Whiten, Lisa Owens, Blair Franklin, and Jabari Lyles.